Make·and·Play

Detectives

Written by
Hazel Songhurst

Devised by
Robin Wright

Illustrated by
Kate Buxton

DERRYDALE BOOKS

NEW YORK • AVENEL, NEW JERSEY

CONTENTS

Produced by Zigzag Publishing Ltd,
The Barn, Randolph's Farm,
Brighton Road, Hurstpierpoint,
West Sussex, BN6 9EL

Edited by Nicola Wright
Designed by Chris Leishman
Photographs by Tony Potter

Color separations by RCS Graphics Ltd, Leeds
Printed by Canale Italy

This edition published by Derrydale Books, distributed by
Outlet Book Company, Inc., a Random House Company,
40 Engelhard Avenue, Avenel, New Jersey 07001

Random House
New York • Toronto • London • Sydney • Auckland

© 1994 Zigzag Publishing Ltd
ISBN 0-517-10222-6

10 9 8 7 6 5 4 3 2 1

ABOUT THIS BOOK

Detectives find out all they can about crimes that have been committed. They search for clues, talk to witnesses, and collect as much information as they can.

In this book, Detective Dan pieces together the puzzle of the jewels stolen from Oakwood Hall. You can help him solve the crime, and make a detective kit of your own to play with.

Step-by-step instructions show you how to make a fingerprint kit for collecting and identifying prints at the scene of the crime. You can also find out how to disguise yourself when you are on the trail of a suspect, test a witness's story with a lie-detector machine, and make a pair of handcuffs to arrest the crimal!

There are tips on how to read body language, and games to sharpen your powers of observation and memory.

You will also find out about the first real detectives, famous storybook detectives, and how science helps today's detectives to solve crimes.

> ⚠️ **Remember that being a detective is dangerous !**
> *Only play detective games with your friends.*
> *Never follow or talk to strangers.*

WHAT YOU NEED

On these pages you can see the things you need to make a complete detective kit and to play the games in the book.

Sponge

Aluminum foil

Face paints

Corks

Plastic pots

Jar lids

Cellophane tape

4.5 volt battery

String

Paper clips

Magazine

Lightbulb

Bulb holder

Large matchbox

Tracing paper

Colored paper

Copper wire

Talcum powder

Elastic

Colored card

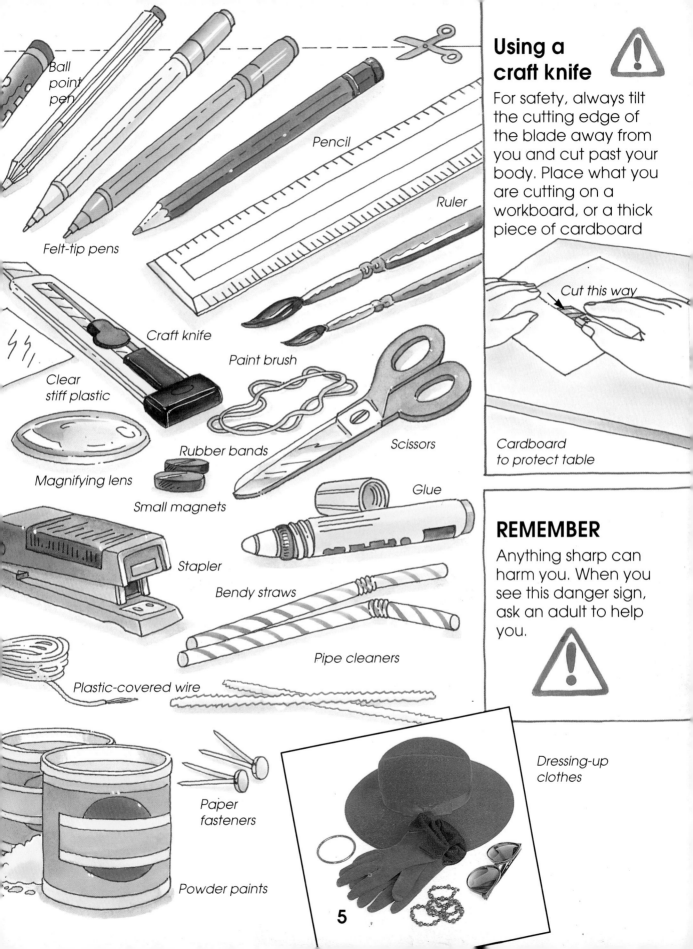

Ball point pen

Felt-tip pens

Pencil

Ruler

Craft knife

Paint brush

Clear stiff plastic

Magnifying lens

Rubber bands

Small magnets

Scissors

Glue

Stapler

Bendy straws

Pipe cleaners

Plastic-covered wire

Paper fasteners

Powder paints

Dressing-up clothes

Using a craft knife

For safety, always tilt the cutting edge of the blade away from you and cut past your body. Place what you are cutting on a workboard, or a thick piece of cardboard

Cut this way

Cardboard to protect table

REMEMBER

Anything sharp can harm you. When you see this danger sign, ask an adult to help you.

THE CASE

The phone rings in Detective Dan's office. He hurries to answer it - perhaps it is another exciting case.

"It's Lady Oakwood," says the voice on the phone. "The family jewels have been stolen!" "I'll be there right away!" says Dan, picking up his ID badge and his warrant card.

Detectives carry identification to show who they are. Make a warrant card like Dan's, giving your name, rank and photograph, and an ID (identity) badge. To make the warrant card, first cut out a $3\frac{1}{2}$in by $2\frac{1}{4}$in piece of stiff cardboard and round off the corners.

Warrant card

$3\frac{1}{2}$in

Colored cardboard

Make a badge from paper or cardboard and glue it on.

$2\frac{1}{4}$in

EDWARD JONES
E Jones

Write your name and official detective signature here.

Cover the front of the card with clear plastic.

Staple the edges together or make a tape border.

Glue on a square of white paper. Stick a smaller square of colored paper on top.

Glue your picture here.

Use a passport-sized photo or drawing.

Make an ID badge

An identity (ID) badge can be worn secretly inside your coat when you go investigating.

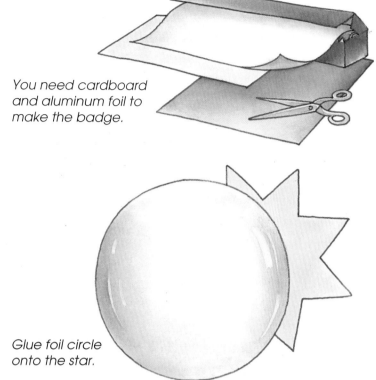

You need cardboard and aluminum foil to make the badge.

1 Trace this star onto cardboard and cut it out.

Glue foil circle onto the star.

2 Cut a foil circle to fit the star. Glue it on to the star.

Make cuts here.

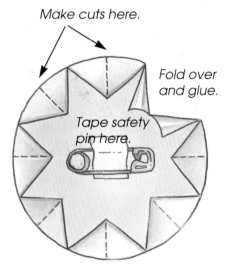

Fold over and glue.

Tape safety pin here.

3 Glue back the foil edges as shown. Tape a safety pin to the back of the badge.

Use an empty pen to score patterns on the star.

You could stick a paper fastener through the middle.

SCENE OF THE CRIME

Dan soon arrives at Oakwood Hall to investigate the case of the missing jewels. He is greeted by Lord Oakwood's new wife, Lady Fenella Oakwood.

Part 1

Lady Oakwood leads Detective Dan to the scene of the crime. The room is a mess. Chairs are knocked over, a window is broken and the wall safe that once contained the jewels is wide open.

Dan looks around him carefully, thinking about what he sees. Then he begins to dust for fingerprints.

Why are the chairs knocked over and the drawers pulled open?

The safe was not forced open.

If the thief got in through the window, why is there no broken glass inside the room?

Taking fingerprints

Keep a record of people's fingerprints - you may need to check them against any you find at the scene of the crime.

1 Press a suspect's fingertip on an ink pad and then onto paper so it leaves a print.

2 Take a print from each of their fingers and thumbs. Label the prints with the owner's name and glue them in a notebook.

Fingerprint kit

Everyone has his or her own fingerprint pattern. Nobody else will have fingerprints exactly the same as yours. That is why prints can be helpful clues. Use this kit to take the fingerprints of suspects and to identify any prints found at the scene of a crime.

Magnifying lens for studying and identifying fingerprints.

Make an ink pad

1 Cut a piece of sponge to fit inside a jar lid.

When not in use, cover sponge with another jar lid.

2 Make "ink" from paint and water and soak sponge.

Fingerprint powder

Powder is dusted onto things to make any fingerprints on them show up. Use darker powder on light things and light powder on dark things.

Make dark powder by grinding a pencil against the blade of a sharpener. Or use dry black powder paint.

Keep powders in a matchbox.

Use talcum powder or a powder puff for light powder.

Cellophane tape for collecting prints.

Collecting prints

1 Brush powder over door handles, glasses, cups – wherever you might find prints. **Ask an adult's permission first !**

2 Make "ink" from paint and water and soak sponge.

3 Press cellophane tape over the print. Peel the tape off, bringing the powdery print with it.

4 Use the magnifying glass to study the print. Does the pattern of lines match any print already in your notebook?

QUESTIONING

To find out what actually happened,
Detective Dan interviews Lord and Lady
Oakwood and their two guests.

*Dan questions them one by one and
writes down everything they say in
his notebook. He also makes notes
about their body language
– the way they behave
under questioning.*

Part 2

Lord Anthony Oakwood

*Upset and shocked.
Saw and heard
nothing.*

Lady Fenella Oakwood

*Discovered the theft.
Calm and dignified.
Saw and heard
nothing.*

Rupert Wright

*Engaged to Laura
Mackenzie. Rather
nervous. Kept biting
his lip. Saw and
heard nothing.*

Laura Mackenzie

*Friend of Lady
Oakwood. Engaged
to Rupert Wright.
Blushed and fiddled
with her hair. Heard
glass breaking in
the night.*

Make a notebook

Make your own
detective
notebook and use
it to note down any
clues you find.
Keep a record, too,
of what people say
during interviews.

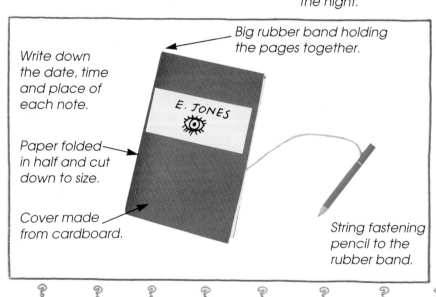

Write down
the date, time
and place of
each note.

E. JONES

Big rubber band holding
the pages together.

Paper folded
in half and cut
down to size.

Cover made
from cardboard.

String fastening
pencil to the
rubber band.

Interviewing

Interview each person separately. Ask them questions. Keep notes of what they say. Study the way they behave to see if they are being honest with you.

Don't forget that a hardened criminal may be very good at deceiving you, and an innocent person may look guilty just because he or she is frightened!

Does everyone agree about the incident?

Does anybody give answers that contradict what the others say?

Does anybody's behavior seem suspicious?

Crossed arms or legs: The person is defensive. He or she may not be telling you everything.

Biting lips: May be afraid of saying too much.

Biting nails or fiddling with fingers: Nervous.

Twiddling with clothes or face: Nervous.

Hands on hips, turning away from you: Defiant and aggressive.

Hands held open with palms upwards: Open and honest.

Leaning towards you with hands clenched : Aggressive and maybe angry.

Lying

If somebody begins to do any of these things while speaking, it suggests they may be lying. Then you could try the lie detector test on p.22.

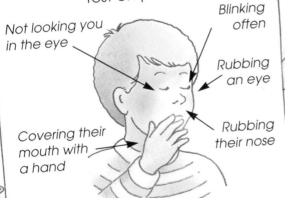

Not looking you in the eye

Blinking often

Rubbing an eye

Rubbing their nose

Covering their mouth with a hand

Observation game

If you are on a bus or train, try to guess the age, occupation and character of some of the passengers. You could even invent a name for them and write a story around their characters.

IDENTIKIT

Next day, Laura Mackenzie - Lady Oakwood's friend - calls to see Detective Dan. She has some important information for him.

Part 3

"I've just remembered something," says Laura. "There was a man – a stranger – near Oakwood Hall the day before the burglary."

" Can you describe him?" asks Dan. To jog her memory, Dan shows her the faces in his identikit file. At last they put together a picture of the stranger.

Different faces

To begin to build up an identikit picture you need to know general details such as the shape of the person's face and coloring.

Then you add details of the person's features, such as nose, eyes and mouth.

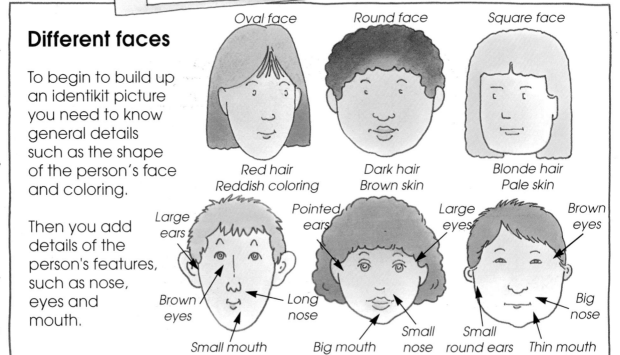

Oval face
Red hair
Reddish coloring

Round face
Dark hair
Brown skin

Square face
Blonde hair
Pale skin

Large ears
Brown eyes
Small mouth
Long nose

Pointed ears
Big mouth
Small nose

Large eyes
Small round ears

Brown eyes
Big nose
Thin mouth

Make an identikit book

Detectives build up pictures of a suspect's face by using witnesses' reports and identikit files.

Identikit files contain hundreds of pictures of different faces. The witness puts together different features, until the whole face looks like the suspect.

Make your own identikit book to help your investigations.

1 Fold four or more sheets of paper in half. Put them together to make a book.

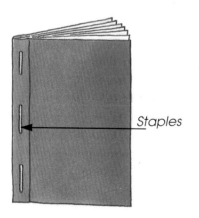

Staples

2 Make a cover from colored paper. Staple the book together.

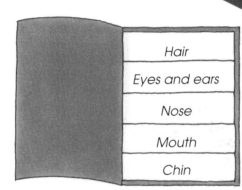

| Hair |
| Eyes and ears |
| Nose |
| Mouth |
| Chin |

3 Cut the pages into 5 strips for hair, eyes and ears, nose, mouth and chin.

Draw a different type of face on each page.

4 Draw a face on the first page. Turn back the strips and draw in different hair, eyes, noses, etc.

COMMUNICATIONS

Detective Dan is looking for clues in the grounds of Oakwood Hall.

He stops outside the summerhouse – there are people talking inside. Putting his ear to the wall, Dan can hear their conversation. He hears a man saying, "I'm meeting him tomorrow in Tony's Café at 4 p.m." At once, Dan telephones back to headquarters.

Make a telephone link

This is an amusing telephone. The sound travels along the string and can be heard in the yogurt pot "receiver."

1 Find two empty yogurt pots (or similar plastic containers). Make a hole in the bottom of each.

2 Put one end of a long string into one of the holes and knot it inside the pot.

String

Knot inside

3 Put the other end of the string into the hole in the other pot and tie a knot inside, as before.

Make a model radio

Bendy straw

Cardboard "buttons"

Large matchbox

Colored paper

Cellophane tape

4 Stretch the string out until it is taut. Take it in turns to talk into one pot and listen in the other.

How far away can you hear each other?

Keep a radio hidden on you for passing messages to HQ.

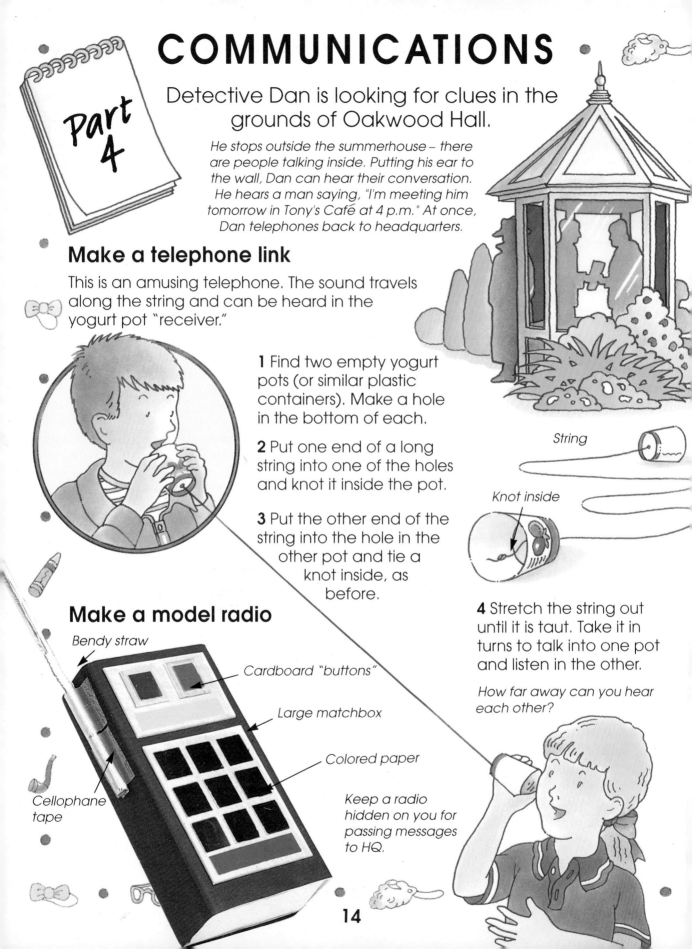

DISGUISE

Part 5

Following the clue he overheard, Dan goes to Tony's Café at 4 p.m. the next day, in disguise.

Rupert Wright comes in and sits at a table with a man whose face seems familiar. Dan watches the men through his special surveillance newspaper. The men swap identical packages and get up to leave. Rupert has dropped a crumpled piece of paper. Dan picks it up – it has a series of numbers on it .

Eyeholes cut in a newspaper help you see without being seen.

Nose and glasses disguise

Fold a piece of thin cardboard in two and trace this shape onto it. Cut it out and open it. Cut out the eye holes.

Cut out and color.

Cut out

Bend back

Fasten elastic here if you wish.

← *Fold*

You can omit the moustache.

Wrinkles made with face paints

Other ideas for disguises

A big hat

Empty frames or sunglasses

Wig or a different hair style

Old clothes

Pillow tied under your clothes to change your shape

LOOKING AT CLUES

Detective Dan studies the clues he has collected so far.

Suddenly, Dan realizes something important: the person Rupert Wright met in the café is the man in the identikit picture! Dan decides to ask the information section at HQ to help find out who this man is. Then a Spottercopter crew report they have just seen the occupants of Oakwood Hall driving away!

An investigation chart

Back at the office, Dan has made a chart to sum up all the clues he has so far. Pin the evidence from your own investigations to a bulletinboard.

INVESTIGATION
Theft of jewels from Oakwood Hall.

Safe was not forced open. The only fingerprints on the safe door are Lady Oakwood's.

Identikit picture of stranger seen near Oakwood Hall matches man seen with Rupert Wright.

Glass found in windowbox, not in room - window broken from inside.

Numbers dropped by Rupert Wright - are they the combination of the safe?

6415
3220

Main suspect: Rupert Wright.

Make a Spottercopter

Here is a fun mobile to make. Hang it in your room to keep watch when you are away!

1 To make the body of the helicopter, cut each end off a bottle cork at an angle, like this:

ASK AN ADULT TO HELP YOU CUT THE CORK WITH A CRAFT KNIFE

2 Glue colored paper over it to look like windows and bodywork.

3 To make the tail, cut a strip of colored paper, about $3/4$in wide. Fold it and glue it to the body, trimming it to make it a bit narrower towards the back.

4 To make the rotor, cut out a circle of acetate or other stiff plastic film, about $2^3/4$in across.

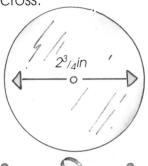

$2^3/4$in

5 Straighten out a paper clip and push it into the cork.

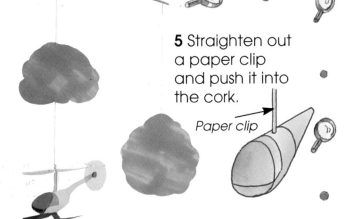

Paper clip

6 Cut a $3/4$in length of drinking straw and fit it over the paper clip. Fix the plastic circle on top.

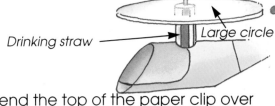

Drinking straw

Large circle

7 Bend the top of the paper clip over into a loop. Hang spottercopter from paper clouds attached to cotton thread and pipecleaner.

8 To make the tail rotor, cut out a small plastic circle and glue a dot of colored cardboard in the center. Glue the plastic circle to the tail.

Colored cardboard dot

Tail

Small circle

9 Trace this shape and cut it out of cardboard to make the skids. Fold and glue them underneath the body.

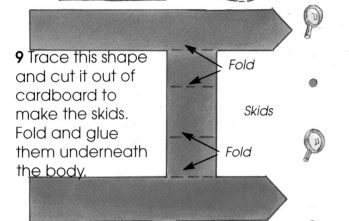

Fold

Skids

Fold

OBSERVATION

While everyone is away from Oakwood Hall, Dan looks for further clues around the grounds.

Behind the house, a muddy shovel is leaning against a wall. Some flowers in the garden have been trampled. In the grass he finds a woman's glove. To avoid spoiling the fingerprints on the glove, he picks it up with a stick and puts it in a plastic bag.

Look and remember

Most people remember very little of what they see. Detectives, however, must watch carefully and notice even the smallest details. The observation games shown here will help you develop your detective skills.

Your move!

1 Make model buildings from folded pieces of cardboard or posterboard. Draw on windows and doors, or cut them out of colored paper and glue them on. Cut out trees, cars and figures from cardboard, leaving a base to fold over (you may need to stick them down with poster-tack).

2 Send your friends out of the room. Arrange the houses, cars and people any way you like.

3 Call your friends in again and give them 30 seconds to look at the scene. Then send them out again.

4 Move some pieces or take a few away. Call everyone back in and see who is first to spot all the changes!

Get the picture!

This is a good party game. Cut out a photo from a magazine. Pass it around for people to study for a short time. Then ask questions about it.

Get everyone to write their answers down. Award points for right answers and a prize for the person with the best memory!

Pictures from a magazine

Witnesses

1 You are the detective. Send your friends out of the room and arrange the scene in any way you like. Make up 10 questions to ask witnesses. For example : 1 What color is the car on the street corner? 2 How many people are wearing red?

2 Bring your friends in. Tell them they are witnesses. Give them 30 seconds to study the scene. Cover the scene (a tablecloth would do). Give everyone paper and a pencil.

3 Ask your 10 questions, and tell your friends to write the answers down. At the end, mark their answers, giving a point for every correct answer. Who is the best witness?

Make buildings, trees, cars and figures out of cardboard or posterboard.

Add any other model pieces you like from train sets or dolls' houses.

Toy figures

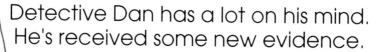

ON THE SCENT

Detective Dan has a lot on his mind.
He's received some new evidence.

Thanks to his researchers at headquarters, Dan knows the name of the stranger in the café. And, at Oakwood Hall, bloodhound Sherlock sniffs the glove and follows the scent trail to the trampled flowerbed. There a package is dug up, wrapped in a silk scarf. There are bank notes inside!

Magnetic bloodhound game

Make a bloodhound for each player and play this seek and score game.

For each dog you will need:
White cardboard, paper
Felt-tip pens
Paper clips
Small magnet
Glue, scissors

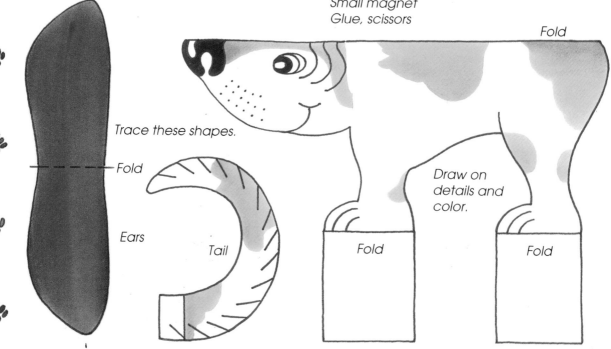

Trace these shapes.

Fold

Ears

Tail

Fold

Draw on details and color.

Fold

Fold

1 Fold a piece of cardboard in two. Trace the dog shape onto it. Cut it out. Do not cut along the fold.

2 Trace the ears and tail onto cardboard. Cut them out and glue them on.

Glue

Glue

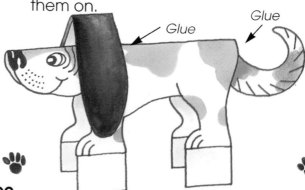

3 Fold the leg flaps and glue them together.

Glue

Glue

4 Glue a small magnet in the bloodhound's nose!

Magnet

You may need to balance the dog with a paper clip on the tail.

To play the game

1 Cut a piece of white paper into at least 20 small pieces.

2 Write a different number on each piece of paper. Use the numbers 1 to 20.

3 Fold each square in half, hiding the number inside. Fasten with a paper clip.

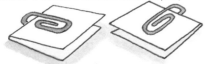

4 Mix all the pieces together on a table top. Take turns pushing your bloodhound out to bring back a piece of paper. (The paper clip will be attracted to the magnet.)

5 When the dog brings the paper "home", open it and look at the number inside. That is your score! When the dogs have picked up all the pieces of paper, add up your scores.

The dog whose owner scores highest is the winner.

THE TRUTH TEST

Now Dan is sure he knows who the real culprit is. But he has to prove it.

Part 9

The glove and scarf found in the garden turn out to belong to Laura Mackenzie. Dan suspects that Rupert Wright was paid to steal the jewels and that Laura, his fiancée, helped him by burying the money he received for doing it. To find out the truth, he questions Rupert using a lie detector.

Q: Did you fake the break-in at Oakwood Hall and steal the jewels?
A: No! (Bulb flashes – a lie)

Q: So you did do it. Was the payment for the robbery?
A: (Reluctantly) Yes.

Q: Did someone tell you the safe's combination number?
A: No! (Bulb flashes)

Q: Another lie. Was it Lady Oakwood?
A: Yes. I admit it.
"I'm arresting you," says Dan. "You'll be charged at the police station."

Do lie detectors work?

Real lie-detector machines measure changes in pulse rate, blood pressure and breathing that may happen to a suspect under questioning. But, as these machines can be unreliable, they are not used in many countries. However, here is a fun one for you to make and play with.

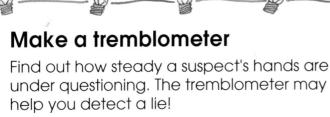

Make a tremblometer

Find out how steady a suspect's hands are under questioning. The tremblometer may help you detect a lie!

You need:
4.5 volt battery
Lightbulb and bulb holder
1 x 8in and 1 x $15^3/_4$in lengths of plastic covered wire
1 x $23^1/_2$in length of copper wire

Bare the ends of the plastic wires about $1^1/_4$in with pliers or scissors.

Wire strippers

Bend the copper wire as shown. Fix one end to a battery connector. You might need to tape this down to hold it tight.

Fix one end of this wire to the other battery connector. Screw the other end to one of the bulb holder connectors.

Copper wire

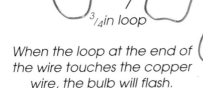

$^3/_4$in loop

When the loop at the end of the wire touches the copper wire, the bulb will flash.

Screw this wire to the other bulb holder connector. Make a $^3/_4$in loop at the other end of the wire.

Screw   *Bulb*

Screw

Bulb holder

If the bulb doesn't light up, check all the connections are firm.

How to play

Here are some games to play with your friends and your tremblometer!

Steady nerves!
See who can pass the loop along the wire fastest without making the bulb light up!

Truth or lie?
Take turns being the detective, asking questions. The suspect must pass the loop along the wire when they reply. If they are lying, their hand may begin to shake, causing the bulb to light up. Of course, their hand may shake if they are simply nervous!

ARREST!

Dan hears that Lady Oakwood and a man are at the airport. He rushes there and meets them just as they are about to board a plane.

Part 10

At the airport Dan arrests and handcuffs Lady Fenella Oakwood, whose real name he now knows is Serena Steel. Dan also arrests her accomplice Hans Zubinsky - the stranger in the café. He was recognized from the identikit picture, and the information about him provided by HQ had included a photograph of his partner - international jewel thief, Serena Steel. Dan had recognized her at once.

To get their hands on the Oakwood jewels, Serena Steel and Hans Zubinsky had worked out a cruel plan. Serena tricked Lord Oakwood into marrying her. Then she invited her friend Laura Mackenzie, with Laura's fiancé Rupert Wright, to stay. Rupert agreed to fake the burglary for a large payment. He then handed over the jewels to Hans, who tried to escape the country with Serena.

Serena Steel
Wanted in several countries for fraud and deception.
Brilliant actress.
Poverty led her into life of crime.

How to make handcuffs

Make these fun handcuffs and use them when you play detective games.

Color the cuffs with felt-tip pens or paint.

You need:

Strong cardboard, preferably corrugated
4 paper fasteners
4 pipe cleaners
Glue
Scissors
Silver foil
Felt-tip pens or paint

1 Trace this half handcuff shape onto cardboard and cut it out. Make three more the same.

Hole here for paper fastener once someone is handcuffed.

Paper fastener goes in here to make hinge.

2 To make the chain, cut four pipe cleaners in half. Roll aluminum foil around each piece. Glue it in place.

Half a pipe cleaner

Foil

Glue here.

3 Bending each piece of pipe cleaner into an oval, loop them together to make a chain. Glue the ends of each oval together.

Glue here.

4 Push a paper fastener into one of the handcuff pieces, at the point shown. Loop one end of the chain over the points of the fastener.

Loop chain on paper fastener.

5 Push the paper fastener into another half handcuff, as shown. Open the fastener out at the back.

Paper fastener pushed through to secure.

Paper fastener

6 Make the second handcuff in the same way and fix it to the other end of the chain. Fasten the handcuffs on your suspect with paper fasteners or tape.

The two halves of the handcuff should be fixed together firmly but able to open and close.

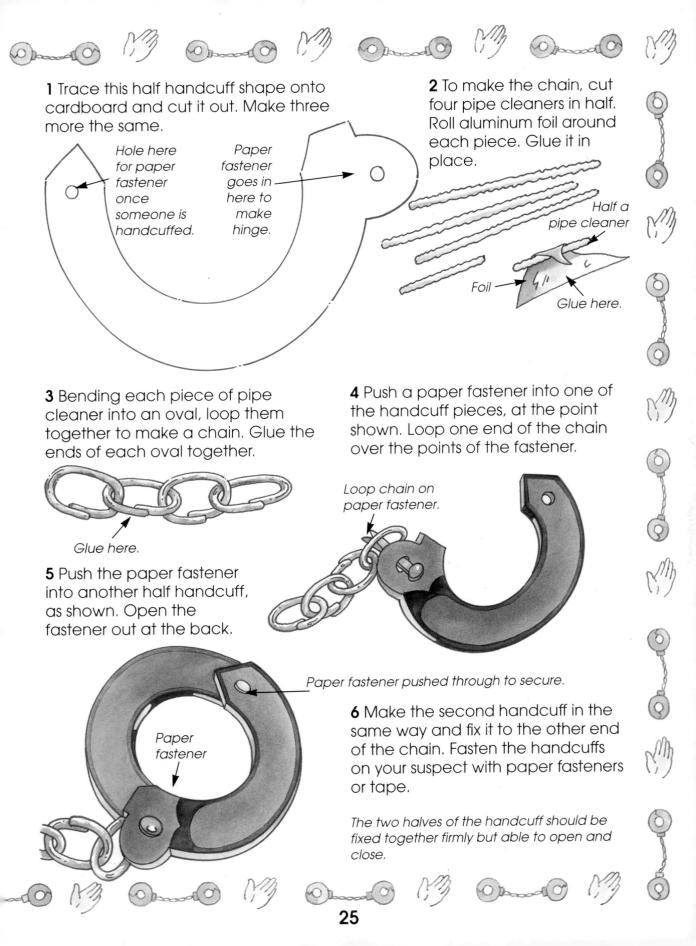

DETECTIVE FACTS

Here are some facts about police forces and detectives in the past.

Before there were proper police forces, **watchmen** guarded the streets at night. Every man over 16 took his turn to be watchman in his neighborhood. Settlers took the system to America and Australia. **Thief takers** were paid to catch criminals. Often they were criminals themselves and were hated by most people.

In 1750, London became the first city to have an organized police force. They were called the **Bow Street Runners.**

In 1829, Sir Robert Peel set up the **London Metropolitan Police Force**. Policemen were nicknamed peelers or bobbies, after their founder.

The first **US police force** was set up in Boston in 1838. It contained just six men.

The Pinkerton National Detective Agency was set up in 1850 in the USA. Early Pinkerton detectives trailed criminals such as the Wild Bunch, and Butch Cassidy and the Sundance Kid. The agency still exists today.

Forensic science

Forensic scientists help detectives by examining the clues found at the scene of a crime. They use scientific techniques to study fingerprints, footprints, clothing, bloodstains, hairs, fibers, specks of dust and dirt, documents, letters and handwriting. The latest developments in forensic science involve studying cells from a person's body. Everyone has their own slightly different cell pattern. This is a very accurate way of identifying a criminal.

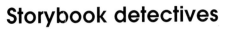

Storybook detectives

Millions of people enjoy reading detective stories. Here are some of the most famous fictional detectives.

Sherlock Holmes
Created by Sir Arthur Conan Doyle. There are 60 Holmes stories in all. The first, *A Study in Scarlet*, was published in 1887. 113a Baker Street in London - Holmes's fictional address - is now a tourist attraction.

Hercule Poirot and Miss Marple
Created by Agatha Christie. Poirot is a short, balding Belgian detective with a little moustache. Miss Marple is an elderly lady living in an English village.

Inspector Maigret
Created by Georges Simenon. This pipe-smoking Parisian detective first appeared in stories in 1931.

Philip Marlowe
Created in 1939 by Raymond Chandler. The cool, witty Marlowe is an American private eye.

Call-up alphabet

Police sending radio messages use a special alphabet to spell out such things as names and car numbers. This makes sure the message gets through clearly and accurately. Use this alphabet to spell out your own message.

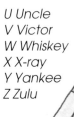

A Alpha	K Kilo	U Uncle
B Bravo	L Lima	V Victor
C Charlie	M Mike	W Whiskey
D Delta	N November	X X-ray
E Echo	O Oscar	Y Yankee
F Foxtrot	P Papa	Z Zulu
G Golf	Q Quebec	
H Hotel	R Romeo	
I India	S Sierra	
J Juliet	T Tango	

DETECTIVE WORDS

Alias A name which someone uses, perhaps to hide his or her real identity.

Alibi Proof that a person was somewhere other than at the scene of a crime when it was committed.

Burglary Breaking into a building to steal.

Charge Officially accuse a person of an offence.

Clue Something that helps solve a mystery.

Detective A person who tries to solve a crime, or carries out secret investigations. Some are plain-clothes members of a police force. Others are private detectives who are hired for a fee.

Evidence Information proving a fact.

Fraud Trickery or cheating.

HQ Headquarters, or main office of an organization.

Investigation An inquiry to try to discover who committed a crime.

Lead A helpful clue or piece of information.

Motive The reason a person has for committing a crime.

Offense A crime.

Robbery Theft using force.

Scene of the crime The place where a crime happened.

Statement A written, signed report by a suspect or a witness.

Surveillance Keeping a close watch on someone.

Suspect A person detectives think may have committed a crime.

Tail To follow someone.

Theft Stealing another person's property.

Witness A person who sees a crime being committed.

Index